Kate—
The Journey

by Kathleen Brooker

PublishAmerica
Baltimore

PublishAmerica has allowed this work to remain exactly as the author intended, verbatim, without editorial input.

ISBN: 978-1-4489-7701-7
PUBLISHED BY PUBLISHAMERICA, LLLP
www.publishamerica.com
Baltimore

Printed in the United States of America

Table of Contents

Kate—
The Journey

A Winter's Night

Crisp air creating shards of diamond dust atop the evening snow.
Radiant heat escapes the eyes to fog the lenses
Lifting the glistens into the air,
Shimmering as they hover
Like fireworks in the summer night sky
Taking a moment to pause…
Before softly nestling back onto the snow.

When I Look at Myself

When I look at myself as the world sees me,
I see a person who lacks
Who lacks beauty
Who lacks grace
Who lacks anything of value to the heart of a man.
I see what the world sees—nothing.

I would give all that I have
all that I am for one person to see me
For one person to love me
for one person to find enough value in me

To want me to see it in myself.

Why?

Why am I always reaching
Beyond where my arms will go?
Why do I keep trying each day
To not let the emptiness show?

Why do I choose to look up
When I know I will see only cloud?
How is it no one can hear
When my heart is crying so loud?

I raise my eyes to the Heavens
For rainbows don't shine on the ground.
I try to put words to my feelings
But no one can hear the sound.

I stretch every part of my being
To a place I have never been
For love must exist somewhere
But who and where, and when?

The Soul

The soul is our innerspace.
From the moment we are conceived
That space begins filling up
First sounds
Then sensations
Then light and air

As we grow, our soul may be
As broad as the horizon, as deep as the sea.
It is filled with the experiences
We have lived, the places we have seen,
The people we are with.

Yet a soul is not something one can fill.
It is not a finite thing but one
Which has a limitless capacity.
As with our muscles, the more we use it
The stronger and larger it becomes.
The more we allow others into our soul
The more space there is.

One would argue that not everyone we allow
Into our soul will stay...this is true.
Not everyone we invite into our soul
Will want to take up residence there...another truth.
Sometimes the only thing that seems infinite
About the soul is its capacity to hold pain,
Yet the pain itself is exercise, and makes us stronger

More flexible, and if we allow, more able to
Understand others' needs, fears, pain.

Generally, people would credit the heart
As the place where love, and pain, resides.
The heart is a muscle that supports the body.
The soul is the essence of who and what we are.

Our souls carry the imprint of all the wonderful people
Who have touched our lives, and the horrible ones.
It does not keep score of the hurts,
Or at least not without our direct intent.
It has extraordinary healing properties
And a never-ending capacity for good,
Again, if we do not get in its way.

While love is the feeling we hold inside of us,
What more is it than an electrical impulse from the brain
That tells us when we are with someone, or thinking of them,
Life seems a little lighter, the sun shines a little brighter.
We smile, we glow, we blush, we sing.

The soul is the repository for all memory, all emotion,
All the faces of our past and, sometimes, the future.
While we feel the affects of love in our chest,
Of attraction in each touch between two
Of like feeling or thought,
These seem to short-circuit the mind and the body
As evidenced in physical and emotional changes…
Appetite, sleep, euphoria,
Increased hormone and neurological response.

Some people seem to pass through this life
Only allowing others to skip across their soul
Like a flat pebble thrown against the
Quiet, peaceful surface of a lake.
Others seek to enrich their souls
By giving of themselves,
Truly caring for and about other people,
Giving them a home in their souls.

Does one love every person who passes their lives,
Albeit for one moment or many decades?
No, not even me.
But that is the goal.
To allow the soul to recognize, as it were,
Things about another that bring us closer
To ourselves.
Help us identify with each other,
Learn, grow,
Seek the equilibrium of a singular humanity.

When and If

When one goes through life without love
They become indifferent to its lack
They go through each day hoping that
Maybe somewhere in the world
There is someone who,
Even if they are unable to
Feel love and attraction independently,
At least will have the capacity
To return kindness for kindness,
Respect for respect.

If someone special comes along,
Someone who pays the least heed
To our existence
Someone who shows a genuine
Affection and friendship
Values us as a person
It awakens not only the need for love
But highlights just how
Deep and empty the chasm.

If they stay
If they continue to show friendship
If they show the capacity to care
The open wound begins to heal
Little by little
From the inside out.

If they go,
Or if we perceive, correctly or not,
That they are unreachable,
The emptiness closes in
In order to try to protect ourselves.
Instead, with the lack of light and air
That their gift originally brought
Loss is all we can seem to see
All we can seem to feel

Then, although they may still
Be only an arm's length away,
The desire to be loved
Becomes almost an obsession.

The relationship between
Reality and perception becomes blurred,
Filled with a desperate longing
That it is only in our minds,
Filled with fear that once again
We are alone.

If My Hands Had Been Touched by God

If my hands had been touched by God
With the ability to communicate
My sight, emotions, perceptions
Into a picture on a piece of paper
What would they draw?

Do you know how when you first open your eyes in the morning
There is a little bit of sleep left in the corners?
It's like He lets us keep just a faint softness as we open to the light
To gently transition us from dream to reality.

Have you ever walked through the grass early on a summer morning
When the dew clings to the blades of grass
As the sun peeks over the hills and the gentle wind blows
Reflecting golden pearls as far as the eye can see?

There is nothing more peaceful than the time just before sunset
With the motion of the water licking at the shore
At the same time softly lulling the gulls and the boats
With the ever changing ebb and tide.

As the sun descends toward the horizon
The lakes and rivers begin to share their warmth with the evening sky
Once again creating that dreamy mist just around the edges of our
vision
As the sun scatters into a million splinters on the surface of the lake
Only to playfully dance, always ahead, until the sky captures

The last rays of the day, painting the sky
With pinks and purples, as soft as a sigh.

God's gift to me, and mine to you,
Does not from my hands arise.
The picture I paint is with my words
Only visible to the mind's eyes.

Don't You Treat Me Kind

If you treat me kind
I'll open up my heart
I'll talk to you like an old friend
And tell you everything.
I'll tell you how I feel each time
Someone has closed me out
When they truly could not do so
Having never let me in.
I'll tell you what I think about
When I'm sitting all alone
Willing to give all I have, and more
And still having no worth.
Do not treat me normal
As I will begin to care too much
I'll allow myself to want more
Than any one can give.
I'll give you all my heart
If you but share just one small cell
I'll yearn to serve you, care for you
If you'll just let me be near.
I'll assume you want to know me
And be a part of my life
You'll be on a first-name basis
With all my children and my folks.

But if you treat me like you should
And keep me in my place
Don't ever let me think you care
Then all will be as it should.

I'll still give you all I have
But expect nothing in return.
I'll be whoever you want me to be
And strive to fill every need.
I've ironed uniforms, I've polished boots
I've left my life behind
For one who was willing to let me love
But never treated me kind.
If I'm with you, I'm not alone
At least not with myself
And I'll be grateful in your shadow
That you allowed me there.
So kindness brings an open heart
But too much baggage besides
So let me in but keep me sound.
Just don't you treat me kind.

How Do I Put on a Page?

How do I put on a page the things that you make me feel?
Words cannot describe the sense of anticipation waiting for your
words to touch my ears.
When we talk, I can think of nowhere else I would rather be
Except maybe where our words would caress each other's ears
with no wires between,
Where I can see the laughter in your eyes and feel the warmth of
your smile.

Your words are sweet. They touch my heart and make it swell
within my chest.
For the first time in a long while, I have dreams, I have hopes.
I do not presume you will love me, but I hope and dream of you
in my arms,
I desire to bring you joy and comfort. I want nothing more.

I know you care about my wellbeing and that I can trust you with
all that I am.
I, in turn, will give you all that I have for as long as I have it to give.
I will give you my heart to hold yours safe, my mouth to tell you
truth, my ears to fulfill your need to share, my feet to walk with
you, my hands to work beside you,
to support you to the best of my ability always.

I will give you my fears to hold until they disappear.
I will give you my tears to wipe away.
I will give you my song to lift your spirit high on the wind.
I will give you all that I have, if you will but only accept my gifts.

Windows

They say the eyes are the windows of the soul.
What would you see if you looked deeply into mine?

Would my heart be bursting at the edges with the love
It waits to find a willing recipient of?
Or would it be small, shriveled, and hard
From all that has been removed without
As much as a kindness in return?

Would my soul be overflowing with faith and hope
In anticipation of a long-awaited fulfillment,
Or would it be black and resentful
Of the degradations it has been forced to suffer?

If you were to look into my eyes,
You would find a child longing to be held;
A teenager longing to be understood;
You would find a young adult bursting with anticipation and
excitement,
Waiting to see what wonders life has yet to hold.

You would see a woman, aged but not old,
A woman with patience learned through waiting,
Faith strengthened through strife,
Wisdom born of experience,
Hope remaining despite sorrows.

If you truly look into my eyes and search my soul,
You will find love, acceptance, kindness, empathy
But you will find so much more.

For you see, I have the capacity to be.
To be anything and everything.
The only limits on me
Are those I put on myself
Or those I allow others to place on me.
More importantly,
Given positive reinforcement and encouragement,
I will grow in every aspect of my being
Becoming more than I ever conceived
Or that the world could ever perceive.

When, not if, you look into my eyes,
My soul will sing you a song
A song of the vision
of a future with no bounds:
No boundaries of time or space,
No limit on love, or kindness,
A beautiful tune consisting of one melody,
Created by the interweaving and harmonizing
Of two lives into one future—
One that transcends humanity.
A love that fulfills and overflows
The breadth of eternity.

Loving You

In the wee hours of the morn
when I wait for sleep to come
my mind takes me on a journey

The journey has no b'ginning
nor has it any end
for intelligence is infinite

Today, my journey is a short one
just over the next hill yonder
to a time and a memory

The time is irrelevant
for this moment is already gone
but memory will e're be ours

This memory is of smiles, laughs,
tears, new hope,
of friends…and more

Giv'n my choice,
would be a cornerstone
for all the memories of tomorrow

A firm foundation to build upon
a lifetime with only one simple goal…
one simple memory…

Loving you…

One

One is an amazing number and an amazing concept.

One is the smallest whole number.
I emphasize the word whole, as it has application in the real world.

We are one person within ourselves.
We are a complete human being
Yet we have the capacity
to take others into our lives
To give up a part of ourselves
To accept that which they are willing to give
In very special circumstances to become
Truly a part of who we are.
Then, although we are one person
The two together create a whole—
One, yet not alone.

Off times, although we choose to share
A part, or all, of ourselves with another
They are unable to reciprocate,
Or they leave.
Although we are still one,
That one seems much smaller,
Somehow less whole,
Less of ourselves
As the part we have given away
remains with them
until such time as healing takes place,
again becoming the smallest whole…
one…alone.

Besides

I always prayed someone would see me
for who I am inside
The gentle, loving soul I have
The humility and pride

My gifts are those you will not see
If looking with your eyes
They are the quiet ones only seen
By one who truly tries

You must look past the face you see
Past the shape and size
To find the woman who I now am
And the child still trapped besides

Can Hope and Depression Co-Exist?

What is hope?
It is believing that there may be a chance, albeit minuscule, that something may improve.
I find that within the grips of depression, hope is hard to find…sometimes impossible.

If I can't see past my all-encompassing chasm of emptiness and pain, how can there be anything else?
I do not hope for "what I deserve," for to my heart I deserve nothing…
So there is nothing to hope for.
I do not hope for love for I do not believe there to be one capable of loving me
Beyond my Lord.
I do not hope for joy, for I receive at least over and again just as much sadness.

When I am able to hope, I hope for safe things…
Balance
An absence of pain
Someone who will allow me to love, of course myself asking nothing in return.

But hope is important.
Hope gives us vision
It helps us to focus our sight and our energy on things outside the hole
It is the finger grip on the edge of the pit that keeps us from falling into severe depression.
It keeps us from giving up on ourselves or others.

Hope is the tool by which we can let in just that pinhole of light which, when allowed,
Can illuminate our souls…
The world still exists outside of our pain.

Hope allows us to see a possibility of that glimmer in ourselves
That the talents we have been blessed with
That the efforts we made are of worth and have not gone totally unnoticed.

If the people who impact our lives have no direct knowledge of depression,
It may be impossible for them to understand.
Its not their fault, but it can still hurt.
We have to allow that their motives are good even though their comments and actions
May not reflect this to us.

One hope that I do have is for my youngest daughter.
She too has suffered from similar issues.
She lost 2 years of educational credit because of fear of school and eventually
Became very close to being a recluse.
Does this relates to hope? Certainly.

Fear, like depression, closes out hope until it creates a dependence on the feeling,
Until the pain and fear become more natural to us than normalcy, in which case,
an actual break must occur to sever the cycle.

In order to accomplish this for my girl, she was enrolled in a Job Corp program
where she has been immersed in the culture of living and learning.
It removed her from her emotional issues and learned habits, and moved her into an
environment where she is responsible for herself, as well as not being able to use her
illness as a crutch.

As she learns the social skills she lacks and a trade, I do have hope that she,
like her siblings, will grow into a mature, responsible adult.
For that, I do hope.

Can depression and hope coexist? They must.
For me, when my depression flares, I hope it passes and I can return to a balance.
When it normalizes, I hope it lasts and am grateful for whatever time that may be.

There is one blessing that I have received…
Because of my "handicap." I am able to feel other's pain, to empathize with
how they feel even if I know nothing about their circumstances.

It helps me to understand love,
The love of my parents,
The love of my children,
The love of God.

Hope is not the absence of challenges, but doing our best to make sure
We do not identify ourselves by those things.

Time to Close This Chapter

I just came from my lawyer's office
Handed over a check
And said, "Time to close the chapter."

Have you ever read a book
That takes you back and forth
Throughout the lives of the characters?
Real life is sort of like that.
Sort of like a book.

Each phase of our lives has its own chapter
Yet each intertwines, interposes itself on the others.

I started this chapter of my life 29 years ago.
It started off on a beautiful, warm November day.
It could not have been more perfect.
Mother nature had saved the prettiest leaves
And the sun shone off of them in all its glory.

In retrospect, would you start the chapter
On the day of your wedding
Or from the moment you first met?
Or would your include that part of your life
In your single days chapter?
In either case, turmoil was never too far away.

The chapter held much change...
Ten moves...
Six children, each of whom have

their own chapter (at least 1 each, anyway).
Was I happy?...I was content...
most of the time.

Somewhere amidst the contentment
And the children and the moves
The antagonist entered
As they always must in any story.

An antagonist can take many forms.
It can be another person
It can be substance abuse
Or personal abuse
Or financial problems
Or illness
Single or multifaceted.

In this case the antagonist
Was/were choices that one
Of the characters chose to make.
These choices resounded
Through my life
And the lives of the children.

It is not one of those situations
Where the offense is clear-cut
Or finite

It started subtly then built
Eventually leading to destruction.

Due to my inability to act
My lack of self-value
My training to be tolerant
And forgiving
And to serve others

It took coming home to find strength
The strength to stand up
The strength to allow myself
To get angry.
The strength to say "No more."

I did.
That was 10 years ago.
My children have continued
With their chapters
Have become wonderful
Young men and women
Many with their own families
And have given me much pride.

Until recently, it never dawned on me
That I too had the right to be happy
I had spent my whole life
Investing all of my energy and love
In the mission of bringing others joy
That I never claimed for myself.

I find now that I am at that closing point
No…a beginning point
Ready to start a new chapter and,
In fact, have found my voice.

You know what?
I have a lot to say
And a talent for saying it
So it seems.

The first analogy that came to mind
Was closing a book
But that is too final
And if each episode of our lives
Is a book unto itself
It can become burdensome to carry.

It is necessary to learn from our past
Allow it to be a part of us
Without identifying with it
to the point that we forget who we are.
We allow ourselves to put away
Those things that bring us joy
And desensitize us to others
Yet forget to allow the things
Of destruction to fade.

So here I stand at the beginning
Again
And I must say I am excited.
So close the chapter
hand me my pen and paper
and don't get in my way
or you might be included
in my next chapter.

Grief Reaction

Life sometimes slaps us across the face...hard
And it hurts like Hell
Sometimes more than we think we can bear.

About 8 years ago, friends lost their
14-year-old daughter in a car accident.
I remember being in the hospital with the mother...
How much pain she was in...
How inconsolable...
How heartbroken.
How she wished she could die too.

This is a grief reaction...
One that we can all understand
And empathize with.
Losing a family member unexpectedly,
Especially a child,
Has to be the worst pain I can imagine.

Do I have to imagine a grief reaction?
No.
Have I lost a child, family member or friend
Tragically? No.
Than how is it that I experience this degree
Of pain?
It is an integral part of my depression.

As I have become older,
Especially over the past 2 years or so,

I have done a lot of introspection
Into my disease
Paying attention to how I feel and when,
To what degree,
Triggers and releases
And the one common thread I find
Is that when I have an emotional issue
Especially when it involves someone
I care about or care for
I experience that degree of distress….
A grief reaction.

    Maybe it is a statement on the
    Degree of which I am capable of
    And choose to love…deeply.
Maybe it is an indication of how
Great my need is to be accepted
By those I care for…
Almost desperate at times.
But for whatever reason,
When I experience feelings
Of perceived rejection…of loss…of fear
It feels as if my whole world has ended.

    It must be noted that whether
    The loss is real or not…
    It is real to me.
    I experience severe pain…
    Yes, pain.
    Not melancholy or sadness
    But a real and true aching
    Throughout my entire being.

With severe depression
People become so immersed
In these feelings of worthlessness,
Of loss,
Of hopelessness
That they do not see anything else.
I am blessed that thanks to my own
Ability to see the 'broader picture'
And with the assistance of medications
I can see ebbs and flows.

    There is no end, nor will there be.
    This is something I expect will be ever present.
    This is my burden, as it were.
    To love too deeply
    And hurt too much.

It does give me an edge though
As I can see both sides.
I can feel and understand other's pain
Yet see that if one does not have
A personal experience with depression
Their own or a family member or friend
They have no frame of reference…
They cannot understand.
Many times, they don't even see.

Rainy Day

I feel a drop on my cheek
Then silence.
There's another on my arm.
They are coming closer together.

I don't see any clouds
But another drop runs down my glasses
(I hate when my glasses get wet.)

I feel cold
And start to sniffle.
I can see droplets on my shirt now.

I remember as a child
Trying to catch snowflakes on my tongue
So of course I have to try to catch a drop.
I catch one running down my cheek.

That's odd…
It doesn't taste like pure rain.
I wonder if the factory has been
Burning rubber or something?
But it isn't an odd taste
In fact it's a bit familiar.
I close my eyes so I can concentrate.
What does it remind me of?

The drops are coming harder now.
I have this large spot down my front.

And my nose is really running.
My cheeks are feeling a bit flush.
I hope I'm not getting the flu.

Another drop falls on my glasses
But it is inside the lens.
I'd love to know how they do that.

I then begin to feel like the proverbial man
With the little black cloud following.
I see other people in the park.
The children are playing.
The sun is shining.
But near me it is cold and wet.

They say if you see the sun shining in a rainstorm
It is going to rain the next day.
I wonder…

Salt! That's what it tasted like…tears!

Perspective on the Fall

Me: I love you, Daddy.

Father: I love you, too.

Me: Daddy, why do I have pain?

Father: Sometimes we have to have pain so that we can appreciate it when we don't. It's called gratitude.

Me: Does everyone have pain?

Father: Yes, but everyone's pain isn't in their body.

Me: What do you mean?

Father: Sometimes their pain is in their thoughts.

Me: You mean I can have pain if I think you're going to spank me?

Father: Yes, in a way, but have I ever spanked you?

Me: No. Am I a good girl, Daddy?

Father: Most of the time. I know that you are doing the best you can.

Me: Do you know what, Daddy? I think I understand. Sometimes when I think of doing something wrong, I get this funny feeling. It helps me remember.

Father: Remember what, my dearest?

Me: That you have told me that I shouldn't do that. Is that pain, too?

Father: That's a way of protecting both you and me.

Me: How does my funny feeling protect you?

Father: If you went ahead and did what I asked you not to do, I would have pain in my heart.

Me: I don't want to make you have pain, Daddy, or make you sad. Is gratitude the only reason we have pain, Daddy?

Father: No, sweet child. When your pain goes away, are you going to remember what it feels like?

Me: Yes, Daddy, though I wish I didn't have to.

Father: And if you saw someone else who had fallen, do you think they might have pain?

Me: Yes, Daddy.

Father: What would you do?

Me: I would run over and make sure they were okay.

Father: Why?

Me: Because when I fell, I was scared. I was all alone, and I wouldn't want the other person to be scared or alone.

Father: That is called compassion. Sometimes we go though pain so that we can help others know they aren't alone.

Me: Like being a good friend, Daddy?

Father: Like being a good friend. When we show compassion, we show love.

Me: So we have pain so we can be grateful, compassionate, and loving?

Father: Not always, but much of the time.

Me: Wow, and all I thought about was my skinned knee.

Father: I understand. Would you like to know a secret?

Me: Yes, please.

Father: When you fell? You were not alone. You have never been alone.

Me: But I didn't see anyone...

Father: Do you know I love you?

Me: Yes. Daddy?

Father: What dear?

Me: Can I come live with you?

Father: Not right away. You have a lot of things you have to do first. But when you come, I want you to live with me forever.

Me: I want that too. Can I ask you one more question Daddy?

Father: Yes.

Me: When I come to live with you...will I be able to see you?

Father: Not only will you be able to see me, but I can hold you in my arms...something I have longed to do ever since you left your Heavenly home.

Me: There is a part of me that knows you are with me, Daddy, no matter how alone I feel, and I know you love me. I will do everything I can, Daddy, to make you proud, because I love you, but can I come home, even if I make mistakes?

Father: Of course, my child. That is why your brother went before you. That is why he died.

Me: My brother died so that I can come home?

Father: He loved you so much, and he wants us to be a family again forever, so he gave up his life, and in taking back his life, he took back yours as well.

Me: Where is my brother?

Father: He is here with me, yet we are both always with you. Sometimes in your life you will feel the need of someone to remind you about me…about your brother…about how much you are loved. That is why you have parents on earth, family and friends. You may find, though, that when you hurt the most, someone will show you the compassion and love that you need, someone will listen, someone will care, just as I hope you learn from your pain and will help me show my other children I love them too.

Me: I will Daddy. Daddy?

Father: Yes?

Me: I love you Daddy.

Father: I love you more.

My Companion

I just realized that I am in what could be considered an abusive relationship. Not only does my companion subject me to total silence, they remind me every minute that I am with them that I am in essence alone, no kindness, no compassion, no connection.

When one is in this situation, one cannot help but believe that they are undesirable or in the very least that there is no one in their life that finds any value in them on a personal level, that sees their worth or wants to be with them. Do you have any idea how much that hurts? It is almost impossible to believe that there is even one person on the face of the earth who is capable of caring about me. That is the message I receive every day.

You may say, "Well, why don't you leave him?" I can't. My companion is an integral part of my life without which I couldn't survive. I would have nothing, be homeless, without a livelihood.

I struggle each day to be able to concentrate on my work, but it is very hard when you are filled with despair. You might think counseling. I am in counseling, but it does not change my dependence on my companion or the total emersion in solitude I feel every day of my life. Sometimes I get e-mails from friends, and that distracts for a little while, but then the emptiness returns and I am again alone for all intensive purposes.

What complicates matters, or what ties me to my companion "at the hip" is that one of my jobs is as a medical transcription, a job that I do from home. One would think that having work would be a distraction from my emotions but, in fact, sometimes they are so strong that I cannot function enough to do my job.

I don't know what to do. I don't know if there is anything I can do. Regardless of how I feel around my companion, as I said earlier, I can't see that my life will ever change and I can't believe anyone will ever care about me, so there you go.

By the way…my companion…

is my computer.

What Do I Want?

So many questions begin with these 4 words...
  What do I want to do?
   What do I want to be?
    What do I want to have for dinner?
     What do I want for Christmas?
      Some "what do I want" questions are obviously
       More important and crucial than others,

But the simple question, "What do I want"
  Defines us...
   Directs us...
    Influences how we treat others,
     How we treat ourselves.
      It also has the potential to empower us.

I have had much contact with many men
  Over the past few years.
   In regard to what they are looking for in a relationship,
    Most say, "I don't know what I want."
     I disagree, or at least to an extent,
      For though they may not know what they do want,
       Their actions reflect a noncommittal attitude
        At any level.

They don't know if they want to be friends.
  They don't know if they want to meet.
    They don't know what they want, yet
      They have no problem with expecting/wanting
        Certain behaviors and freedoms
          With no strings attached.
            Sounds to me like they know what they want.

Back to the question…What do I want?

What Do You See?

What do I see when I look at you?
I see a man who has touched my heart.
I see a man…a good man.
I see a loving father.
I see a man with great passion.

I see a man who has allowed himself
To become complacent
yet has so much potential.

I see a man who has a vision
Of what he wants and
Where he wants to go
But has either simply lost his momentum
Or has forgotten how great an effort
Is needed to receive
A great reward.

I see a man who despite his
Exceptional communication skills
Chooses not to talk…
A man who with all his education
And life experience
Chooses not to make informed choices…
A man who has known loss in his life
Yet feels no need to hold close
Possibly his one best chance
For happiness here on earth
Or in Heaven.

I see a man who
I could have been content
Spending eternity with
But who has chosen
To let today pass
With a disclaimer of "maybe tomorrow."

I see a man who I ought not want
In my life…
Who has little to nothing to offer me
Who cannot take care of himself
Not to mention supporting me
Even on simply an emotional level,
Who shows no vesting in me,
My life, my wants and desires…
Or in us.

Yet, I see a man who I could love
With all my heart.

What do you see?

I don't know. You have never told me.

Words on a Page

I have in front of me words on a page.
They were a gift given with love.
They represent all that is good
In a man who is able to see me
Which is as it should.

He tells me that life without me in his arms
Is not worth money or fame.
He offers his shoulders…he offers his heart.
He offers his home to me
Yet we are apart.

The words bring to mind a life with this man
Filled with beaches and sunshine and him.
The warm ocean breeze that will caress my brow
The comfort of his arms…
I wish I could feel them now.

He offers to me all that he has
His earthy goods, comforts; his time.
We'll fly to new heights
We'll walk hand in hand
He'll love me with all of his might.

Does he know that my heart already is his?
Does he know that it sings with his name?
Does he know that he is the only one
Who my soul recognizes
Whose true love he's won.

Across all of the nation, over oceans and seas
He carries it with him held dear
This wonderful man, he holds the key
The only thing left to him
Is to come and claim me.

I have in front of me words on a page.
They were a gift given with love.
I'll read them each day while he's afar
I'll pray that his travels are safe
And soon he'll return to my arms.

A Star

1
The sun circles the earth
Or so it seems.
When it comes,
Do we realize the gift
We have received?
Or do we go through life
Taking for granted
The sweetness and warmth
Held within?

2
We see it come from the east
Each day
And when it leaves us,
Others share it's presence.
Ever wonder whether it shines
On those you love
Or whether there is a space of
Darkness between you,
If only for a second of time?

3
As I stand facing east
Looking into the morning sun
I wonder how many times
My love felt the sun

On his face that day
Let it warm his skin
And wished I were there.

4
The love of my life stands on a shore
Looking into the setting sun
Wondering whether when it arrives,
At the point in time that I will see it,
Will I be thinking of him,
Knowing that he sent me a star
To share his light and his love
To warm my heart…
And my day.

A Gift Not Taken

The other evening, my sister looked at a check I had given her, then picked up off the kitchen table an envelope my mother was mailing. She seemed to be studying the two documents closely then noted that that the handwriting looked very similar, which I took for a compliment, as my mother always had had lovely writing.

When I was a young teen, mom offered to help me learn how to write attractively. Of course, my belief at the time was why bother? Writing is writing, and I intended to do the least amount as possible, especially not PRACTICE. I had enough of that when she made me take piano lessons. I will admit that the torture was distributed evenly, as all of my siblings had lessons as well. I blame my oldest sister for the whole mess. Deb was 7 years older than I and actually had a natural talent for piano. Maybe it was because she had long, lovely fingers (then again, Deb was lovely in all ways, other than her Italian temper). Of course, it was the attitude that if Deb could play so well and I couldn't, then I wasn't practicing enough. So I bid "No, thank you." to mom for the penmanship lessons and went on my way.

Years later, after I was wiser and quite old—probably a whole 30—I became interested in calligraphy, the beautiful lines, classic styles, so I bought myself a kit. Just a basic one with a booklet demonstrating the letters of about 6 different styles of writing. And guess what…I practiced. Just off an on, when time allowed in between changing diapers, making meals, caring for the house, church responsibilities. Of course, as most things go, life interfered and the pen was set aside, likely left behind in one of our moves.

Although I never used the calligraphy to the extent that it became a skill, I still enjoyed putting a little flag on my letters or an extra curve here and there. It added a little something. Studying the patterns, though, did affect my overall handwriting, especially my signature, which I take now pride in.

I once interviewed for a job at the college where I work, which I did not obtain. A few weeks after, I passed one of the faculty members who had been on the interviewing committee. He told me he was sorry that I had not gotten the job but that he felt that I had very good interviewing skills, which made me feel good. But what made an even greater impression to my mind was his following comment, "Did you take calligraphy? You have beautiful handwriting!" Funny how the small things we do in life make a noticeable difference.

So here we sat at my mom's kitchen table some 35 years later. I realize now that my mom offering to work with me on my handwriting was not a criticism…it was a gift she lovingly offered. I have a feeling that had I accepted her time and her patience, those would have become special memories, likely ones I would have recalled over and over through the years, instead of a single thought of sitting at the kitchen table having arrived at the same destination, with the gift of those memories not taken on the journey.

Tears

I read somewhere that tears are a sign of anger.
Some of us were taught that it is not acceptable
To show our anger or irritation with others.
We are taught in church to turn the other cheek.
So where does that energy go if we do not allow
It to express itself?

We internalize it…we "suck it up."
We hold the anger in and it becomes pain.

If someone hurts someone we love
Then it is okay to be protective
And lash out.
If someone hurts us, we simply hurt
There is no one there to protect us
Or at least cares enough to do so.

If someone rejects those we care about
We show compassion, kindness.
When we are rejected, or perceive rejection
We hold our pain as close as we can
So no one will see our shame.
As Long As Kate Is Somewhere In There To Be Found
(I think someone finally understands)

I know full well that our love is real
To both of us
I know that he is a good man
And he truly cares about me.

But throughout my life,
I have often wondered if love would be enough.

When one suffers from mood swings,
depressive episodes, severe spells of grief
It is almost impossible not to be swallowed up
By the havoc that is being wreaked upon one's psyche.

I have noted in my disease a pattern
Where periods of perceived silence become so loud
That they literally absorb all my love and my hope
And turn it into pain and fear
Into the feeling that I have once again lost everything I hold dear
And am unequivocally and irrevocably alone...forever.

Although I know these feelings are based in my illness
And not in any preponderance of truth
I nevertheless cannot stop them, control them, or reduce them
Until the cycle plays itself out
And I am again restored to normalcy.

I do not become my disease.
My disease becomes a wall around me
Through which I cannot break
For a time.
It controls my thoughts, my actions and reactions.

In my desire to gain better control of my emotional health
I have spent literally years tracking my own symptoms,
Noting the times, the triggers
Anything that can reduce the severity or length of the attack.
I have also come to the realization that this curse will be with me
For the rest of my life, to one degree or other.

In most all of my previous relationships, mostly simple friendships,
I have been open and honest with the other party from the start,
Wanting them to be forewarned and prepared for the inevitable.
Trying to protect them from investing themselves unknowingly
In a relationship that may prove to be more intense
Than they have a desire or the capacity to function within.

There have been those who decided up front
They were not willing, or did not see a value in me
Worth putting forth the effort to have in their lives.
And there have been those who have chosen to take advantage
Of my emotional state
To make me believe they cared
While simply serving their own ends.
I believe that was their loss…every single one of them.

My darling has been through almost all spectrums
Of my disease in the past four months
From a caring friendship to my backing off to protect him
From my moodiness
From again building toward a common unity
To becoming paranoid and distrustful
And walking away from my dearest friend.

A simple Christmas wish reopened the door between us
And we began again.
Picking up like we had known each other forever
And our friendship has blossomed
Into a love truer than I had ever hoped.

I have had multiple cycles since Christmas,
All triggered by silence and misperceived rejection.

During these times, and throughout the healing process
I have done my best to be open and honest with him
About what I am going through, how I feel and
Have plied his mailbox with letter after letter
Of all of these feelings, concerns, thought processes.

Following one of these episodes
And the subsequent communicative healing process,
I received an e-mail from my love commenting
On the number of communications he had received.
Then, he made a singularly poignant comment
That will stay with me forever, and I quote,
"…as long as Kate is somewhere in there to be found,
I will be here searching for her."

With his one comment, he has proven to me
That love is enough
But only when love is truly given with a full heart
And when the heart recognizes that there is beauty
Even within a realm of pain.

Yes, Kate is in here somewhere

and loves you with every ounce of her being.

I can finally say, "I know someone understands."

I Need Him

My love says that I need him
My heart says this is true
I need him more than sleep at night
And more than morning dew
I need him more than life itself
For should that flame go out
I'll need him through eternity
Of that, I have no doubt.

My love knows that I want him
To share our lives every day
To enjoy the special things that come
Together, work and play
I want him in the sunshine
To walk hand and hand in the rain
I want him to be next to me
To share his joys and pain.

No greater love has any
Than for this man have I
My heart is full, my spirit sings
My soul it soars on high
I love him more than want him
I want him more than need
I need him more than I can say
Oh come, my love, to me.

Letters I Will Never Send

I sit in silence
Writing letters I will never send
The pages filled with sorrow
The sheets stained with my tears

I feel like I have lost my best friend
I can't see you
I can't touch you
I can't hear you
You haven't moved
But you are no longer here with me
And the empty space in my heart
Is swallowing me whole.

I try to fill the void with words
To help you understand
How pain fills my being

I try to fill it with love
But each time I turn my back
Love escapes me

I want so to fill it with trust
But too often the fear overshadows
All of your words when
I can't see you
I can't touch you
I can't hear you.

I sit in silence
Writing letters I will never send
For I fear that my doubt and pain
Will truly cause you to go.

My Heart Is Soaring Tonight...Literally

My heart is soaring tonight...literally.
It is leaving from Washington
And flying all the way to Hawaii.
Then from Hawaii to Korea.

One would ask how a heart
Could fly when its body
Is aground in New York.

I gave my heart to someone special
So he would not be alone on his long flight.
He placed it carefully and gently into
His left inside jacket pocket
Where it fit perfectly
(A heart is only as large as our fist...
did you know that?)

As he travels, my heart will lie
Next to his chest
Warm
Soft
And if he listens very quietly
He will hear my heart
Beating in time with his.

My heart is soaring tonight...literally
Although my physical heart
Has not left my body
The love that it holds

Is safely tucked in the heart and soul
Of another.
So as my love flies
Will my heart.

And when he returns to me
My love will truly find his home
In my arms
And our hearts will soar…literally.

Bidding the Sun Adieu

On an afternoon flight to Phoenix,
Heading west,
The sun was at about a 20-degree angle
With the plane.

As I watched,
I would see little glimmers of yellow
Showing in the clouds
Below where the sun shone.

As we got closer,
It would disappear
But if I was lucky,
Another would be born
To attract my attention
In a slightly different direction.

When the sun was just sitting
On the front edge of my window,
I lay my head so it was lighting
The right side of my face
And I slept peacefully and happy.

When the sun at last was just beyond
My view around the corner of the window,
I awoke and noticed a lovely sunset...
Or so I thought.
I'd look, admire, doze, and awaken
To appreciate the beauty once again.

Ever so often during the flight,
I would look down to see whether
I could see the ground
Instead of the clouds.
The earth actually looked brown,
No longer the white
Blanket of pristine snow
That covered the east.

As I looked up
And again beheld the sunset
In all its oranges and yellows,
I realized that the sun, in fact,
Was not on the horizon yet.
In glancing as far as my head could turn
To see out of this 8" x 12" oval
They call a window,
The blueness of the sky
Became warm, inviting.

At that moment,
My eyes moved down
To the fine line where the
Sky met the clouds.
There I found more than beauty
but what I consider a natural wonder.

Running along the horizon
From the southeast to the southwest
And vice versa
Was a bow of color
Encircling as far
As my gaze could see.

At first, what was only
Soft hues of yellow and orange
Now flamed with red below
And vibrant green above,
Blending gently into the azure sky.

As the sun descended
To the edge of the clouds
And started to set,
The prism effect was lost,
The green fading
As the sky separated
Into a soft baby blue
Next to the still present
Warmth of orange and red
With the sky above taking
On the tone of violet
That had been missing
From the encircling
Bow of colors…

With a crimson streak of cloud
Bidding the sun adieu.
The Parachute…Right?

One day I jumped
Out of a plane at 39,000 feet.
I had a good, sturdy parachute
And you were jumping with me,
So all was okay…right?
Wrong!

I had never jumped before
And when I looked for your hand
To help me with the rip cord
You weren't there.
I looked all around.
I could not even see the plane
I had jumped from.
Tragedy…right?
I didn't jump from a plane.
I did something much more dangerous…
I fell in love.
You asked me to not doubt
Your love for me…
I came to trust you.
You said you'd protect me
When I was afraid,
That you'd hold me
Until life made sense again.
I wanted nothing more
In the entire world
Than to spend the rest of my life
With you…
So I jumped.

We planned a vacation,
You and I…
Nine days together
To get to know each other better,
Discuss our future,
Make plans.
I took off time from work,
Even losing income

To have this precious time
With you.
Then something horrible happened.

The day you were to fly in,
You agreed to call me when you landed...
You didn't.
I was so sick with worry
That something had happened to you,

I broke.

I survived the next day in silence,
Figuring you got busy,
But you would be there Friday
When I got home,
As that was when we
Were supposed to fly away
Into the horizon together.

Silence, absence.

Although I found out by a twist of fate
Days later that you had fallen ill,
No word from family
Or those who worked for you
That you were unable to come.
Nothing.
Which is what I felt like...
Nothing.
If I am always on your mind,
Did you think of me crying?

Did you understand that
With the silence,
My entire life,
My future
Seemed gone?
I feel like I jumped from the plane.
I feel like I was falling and
The one I had trusted
To protect me had a hand
In pushing me out,
Leaving me to whatever
Fate befell me.
One may say that nothing
Could feel as bad as falling
From 39,000 feet alone,
No parachute…right?

Wrong.

At least then,
I'd know the pain would end

I Ran Away

I ran away
I could not stay
The pain was just too great.
You were gone
You had moved on
Solitude my fate.

I sat and cried
And thought of you
Our life that was to be,
Of lost hope
And shattered dreams
No more in store for me.

It seems no matter
How great my love
Or how much I give of myself,
It's ne'er enough
To secure a heart
Of one such as yourself.

I flew away to a far shore
To hide my face in shame
To separate my poor heart
From the ever burning flame
A flame that not so long ago
Burned brightly with your love,
Now singes the edges of my mind
Like the slapping of a glove.

The coast was warm
The breezes cool
The ocean's gentle sounds
Soothed my soul
Calmed my heart
The sun shone brightly down.

Yet when my days were quiet
And my thoughts would turn to you
My heart still wanted
The same things,
My love, to be with you.

Soon I will return
From whence I came
To family, work, and son
And though I cry
For want of you
Still I must go on.

I ran away
To escape
The pain of wanting you
But what I found
Was that here or there
My heart must still be true.

So I'll hold onto hope
Even tho in vain,
That you will return to me
To heal my soul
To make me smile.
My heart, dear one, is thee.

The Trouble with Flying

The day starts bright and cheerful. I am on time and ready, plenty of time before the 7:30 shuttle I had scheduled to take me from the hotel to the airport. As I grab my bags and enter the elevator, I have no clue of the day that awaits me.

I have scheduled my trip to visit friends in California with a 2-hour layover in Phoenix to visit my daughter and her husband. I am grateful to have been able to do so and looked forward to a long, busy, but rewarding day.

When I arrive at the concierge desk to check out, I ask how soon the transport shuttle that I had scheduled the evening before will be leaving. I am informed that it has already departed and will not be back until about 8:30. As I stand at the counter about to have issue with the clerk, my cell phone rings. My mother relates to me that US Air has cancelled my flight between Philadelphia and Chicago. By this time, I am beside myself.

I phone the number US Air has left with my parents, only to reach the last person I ever want to talk with on this or indeed any day—an automated, prerecorded system message. I go back to the desk and ask if they have the number to US Air—they do not. The clerk is kind enough to go find the number to the airport…progress, at least.

I go sit down in the hallway by a desk with chairs at either end…one of those long dark tables in front of a mirror, right across from the elevators, with a vase of flowers in the center. Don't get me wrong…I love flowers…but I am so upset by now that I don't even pay attention to whether they are real or plastic, or even what type of blossoms they are. I do love the fact that the mirror is centered on the elevators so that travelers can do one final check on their appearance before proceeding on to their dates, appointments, or travel. Talk about encouraging vanity!

Back to US Air.

I once again get an automated system message but after a few redials am finally able to maneuver my way through the web of yeses and noes to a live human being—probably the one token person they still have on their payroll. She even almost speaks English and does her best to help rework my schedule. The best offer she can make is a flight to Philly then a direct flight to LAX, totally removing Phoenix, and my daughter Esther, from my trip.

At this point, I am VERY grateful not to be sitting in front of the mirror, as tears are freely flowing, like they will wear away my skin into permanent crevices against a face turned stone in grief.

She keeps looking and...hallelujah...does find a flight plan that meets my needs...1 pm out of Albany; 3:36 out of Philadelphia; 2 hours in Phoenix then on to LA. I go back to the front desk and ask about the shuttle. The young clerk, who has been very patient with my rantings, says he can/will schedule it (correctly this time), so I request it for 10:30, leaving a generous amount of time at the airport for "pleasantries." The clerk gives me another room key so I can "rest." I take advantage of their "hot" breakfast offerings (though I should have passed up their not-so-well-done bacon), then went back to my room and lie down until 10.

At 10:15, I am again in the lobby and within 5 minutes the van has pulled in, as promised, and I am on my way. At the US Air counter, the clerk advises me they are moving me to an earlier flight to Philly. Sounds okay to me…less time waiting in NY, one step closer to my girl. 10:30 comes and goes. Seems that although the weather where I am is decent, Philadelphia has all sorts of flight delays due to winter weather, so though our plane sits just outside the terminal, within immediate reach, they will not let us take off. As the morning wears on, I sit there, the frustration waxing and waning, the tears and pain coming and going like waves upon the sand, unpredictable, sometimes so gentle they are hardly there, at times slamming against my heart so greatly I want to run, but I know I must get to Esther.

For some reason, I have made an emotional connection between this trip and my mental stability, which of late has been somewhat tenuous.

Afternoon comes, and it begins to look like the flight I was originally scheduled for at 1 pm will arrive before this one takes off. The ladies at the flight desk begin looking at people's schedules and switching them to alternate flights. When it looks like neither of the 2 flights to Philly will arrive in time for my Phoenix connection, I am called up. Once again, an alternative route is proposed—this time Albany to Charlotte then on to LAX.

I relate, as before, through bitter tears and frustration, my need to stop in Phoenix to see my daughter who is 3 months pregnant. The clerk reminds me, as had the operator weeks ago…no…that was just this morning…that the airline's only obligation is to get me to my final destination. I have to hold onto the thin thread of hope that I can still make it to Phoenix, so I have her switch me back to my original flight, expected to leave first, with the agreement that if it does not take off by 2, I will then take the Charlotte flight; I return to my seat.

Within 10 minutes, I am standing outside in the wind, waiting to board the plane. My scarf blows off! What next!!! A gentleman behind me dashes forward and grabs it, returning it safely to my possession. As I get on the plane and take my seat, I experience a feeling of relief, like a warm ocean wave flowing over me. Now I can relax and enjoy the rest of my trip.

Except…as soon as the dozen or so passengers board the plane (which, BTW, the clerk initially told me was full), they decide the 10:30 flight is going to leave first. I, as well as the other dozen or so passengers, off-board and cross the windy yard to the other aircraft, this time my scarf well in hand.

Why Can't I See? Blindness

There is a part of me that, when I fall in love, becomes blind.

This does not sound out of the usual, does it?

We blind ourselves to other's faults, their looks, their shortcomings, their inabilities.

But my blindness goes much deeper.

When I love someone, I cannot see him as an addition to my life…he is my life.
I can no longer see my life without him.

I want what he wants.

I see myself only as his wife, and all other aspects of my life…
who I am…the things that make me unique and special…
are pushed to the back of my mind, my life.

The true blindness is that I cannot see that I have become so obsessed…not in the sense of becoming unable to function on a day-to-day basis, but more that any plans for the future are based in my life with that person, and when anything happens to question or threaten that perception, I break, literally…

For when my loves is gone, so is my heart…my life.

Only after there is healing can I see that the obsessive nature was there.

You would think I, as many times in my life I have had this same reaction,
would be able to see it, somehow prevent myself from vesting so completely in the feelings another offers me...the life, the love, the protection from myself...that I truly become nothing, so that at the point they leave my life, or I perceive any anger, rejection or termination of the relationship, I am empty...I am nonexistent.

I suppose that the nothingness already exists as a part of me, unfortunately a big part.

I want/need someone to value me before I can value myself.

Sometimes I can see all the gifts that I have been given...my talents, my children, my parents and siblings, job security...but when I find someone who offers me even the smallest part of their heart, their hand, their life, I become blind to myself and can only see them.

I recently experienced such a love...and such a loss.

It devastated me.

Although I am now on the outside and can see, and can put this and so many other relationships into perspective, there is still pain, but it is no longer all-encompassing.

Do I still love him? Yes. But now, I love him as an external being, not a part of me.

Maybe I cannot love myself except through the eyes of others, and that is why I cling to the smallest show of compassion or acceptance.

Unfortunately, sooner or later, it ends, and the chasm grows deeper,
at moments feeling impossible to see any way out
and feeling like it will consume me.

I hope someday to be able to see that part of myself, to reconcile with my past,
to be able to have a relationship where I am an equal—
in my own mind more than theirs.

I want to know why I am blind.
I want to see my own value.
I want to be able to be an asset to another's life,
But I want them also to be an asset to mine.

I know myself well enough to know that I have a vast need for external approval

I don't demand one's best, only their acceptance.

I need to find that place in me where this blindness exists
and open it to light and healing.

Otherwise, I will always be subject to my needs and
never able to seek what is best for me…
Only seeing the one in front of me…

Never able to see myself.

Fear

The first time that I remember being truly afraid for someone, I was 14 years old. My boyfriend, Johnny, a boy whose family bought a house in town for vacations, and our neighbor DJ had taken off, before I arrived at DJ's house, to run a race around the one block in our town. DJ's mom, brothers and sisters, and other neighborhood children sat on their front porch awaiting the winner. We saw DJ turn the corner at the top of the street and come into the "home stretch," about halfway down the block. DJ arrived all out of breath and said Johnny had fallen, and he thought his leg was broken...or was it his arm? I immediately took off running at a full clip, though I had never been athletic. I ended up coming full circle around the block, only to find Johnny sitting on DJ's porch holding onto his arm as if it were broken. He looked at me and winked. One would have thought I would be relieved to know it was a jest and he was joking. Not me.

That intense fear shattered something inside of me. I was in a state of breakdown. I could not stop crying. I had planned to sleep out behind another friend's trailer that night and already had my sleeping gear out. Although Johnny did come to where I was staying and tried to talk to me, he had no way of coping with my distress and left. Neither Susan, DJ's sister, or Mike, a friend, probably my best friend growing up was 3 years my younger and only summered in our town, know what to do, but Susan and Mike stayed with me. They stayed through my crying. Through my taking 3 beers from my dad's basement refrigerator and drinking them, through my lying down on Main Street hoping to be run over, and from which they pulled me away. I don't remember much more of the incident/evening other than getting in trouble with mom a day or 2 after (I don't remember which of them told).

Later that summer Judy, a very attractive girl, came to stay with her grandmother. She and Johnny became friends, and I was worried about her taking him away. I remember one day heading down the tracks to run away, again having such intense pain because of my own fear/perceived rejection, broken and shamed. Judy made Johnny stop me from leaving. Although I kept walking and refused, he grabbed my arm and physically pulled me back toward town until I stopped resisting, the tears still flowing like a waterfall.

The second came with Kevin, my first real boyfriend, my first fiancée. We had met and started dating during my first year at college. I applied for a 1-year leave of absence to live with my grandparents in the middle of nowhere, caring for my grandmother with Parkinson's disease. The summer was great and Kevin spent quite of time with me at the farm. That fall, Kevin began not showing up when he said he would be over. I remember vividly sitting on the edge of my bed in the dark, staring down the hill into the blackness of the night. The only thing my mind could imagine was that he had an accident and was lying in a ditch dead or dying. Again, this fear would seep into my bones, and I would cry uncontrollably.

The next spring, Kevin joined the military the end of February. I went to stay with Deb, my oldest sister, over Easter vacation to help care for her daughter. One day, Deb took me to a pay phone and we called home. My mom had the distasteful job of telling me that Kevin had married his ex-girlfriend in mid March before leaving for basic training.

I broke. I could not believe it, though I had lived in fear of losing him since before Christmas, doing my damnedest to hold onto him, desperate, sacrificing all that I had, all that I was. After crying constantly for a couple of days, I told Deb I needed to go home, so they took me to the Greyhound station. When I got home, I bought a bus ticket to Chicago. I had to talk to Kevin. It wasn't true. It couldn't be. He loved me. I had to see his face and talk to him. I left my parents a note and got on the bus, which was supposed to take me to Binghamton. We got about 30 miles from Binghamton when the bus broke down. It seemed like hours before the replacement bus came, and by the time I arrived in Binghamton, I had missed my connection. The ticket agent told me I could get a connection in Syracuse, so there I went.

When I arrived, there were a few hours before the next bus left, so I phoned my friend Terri, who picked me up and brought me to her parent's house. I thought it would be considerate to phone my parents to let them know I was in Syracuse and okay. My dad tried to talk me out of going, if for no other reason than Chicago was a rough city at that time, but I had to go. He told me if I insisted on going he would fly out and meet my bus when I arrived. That small token of concern and self-sacrifice was enough to break the obsessive spell that had come to control my mind and heart, though it could not heal the pain.

The only other true fear reaction was last week, but a little history. He had introduced himself on the internet in late September. All I had said I was interested in relationship-wise was friendship. We began a conversation and became good friends. At one point, I knew I was becoming more attached to him than was healthy, and I told him I needed to stop chatting for a while…didn't know how long. He accepted this graciously, and we parted. At some point later in October, or early in November, I think, we began again. We got to the point where he indicated he wanted me in his life. As I had asked for pictures of him, he had sent me a couple of he and his sweet, now departed wife. He also sent others of his house, his boat and his plane. Everything was okay until we parted for the night. In the silence, I became paranoid. I examined all of the photos with an eye for inconsistencies, finding many, and basically accused him of thinking I was stupid and lying to me. Within a day or 2, I was back to normal. I apologized but also gave him the advice to "cut and run" from me, so we again left things be.

About a week before Christmas '08, I came across his e-mail, so I e-mailed him, simply wishing he and his son a Merry Christmas. He responded, and we were able to put the incident behind, once again able to enjoy the open communication we had shared. During that time, there were many "spells," and he came to be very understanding and supportive of me. Just after Christmas, our relationship blossomed into a romance and he committed to protect me, as well as love me to the end of time. Once he expressed his feelings for me, I allowed my heart to open and accept his love, coming to love him more than my own life. Over time, plans were made for him to pick me up and we would spend a week together to get to know each other face to face, make plans for our future, walk hand in hand. We had already talked marriage. Due to family commitments in Korea, he was not going to be able to arrive in NY until the Wednesday before we were to leave. I had an e-mail from his son after his departure. His plan was to land in NY at 11:30 am. As the afternoon wore on and I received no word of his arrival, the fear for him grew. I didn't have to work that evening, so those precious hours were to be ours to spend together. After hours of building concern and total silence, I once again broke. I checked my computer once again at 6 pm. I couldn't stand being in the house, so I put on my boots, coat and scarf and walked out into the night, into the freezing rain. I didn't care. I walked out of town. My sister who had driven by forced me to take her flashlight, a heavy metal one that made whichever hand I had it in cold and painful.

I continued on, stopping about a mile from town, turned my back to the road and just stood there sobbing, praying to God for his safety. I knew something was wrong, but I had no way of finding out what. It took at least an hour before I could even think about returning to the house where I would again be consumed with checking my e-mail and waiting for one word of his safety.

When Friday came, I did my best to hold onto one shred of hope that he would be there when I got home from work. He wasn't. Now disappointment and sadness piled in on top of the fear and worry. Only through a twist of fate did I find out that he was in the hospital, but I had no way of communicating, so the frustration kept building. I called every hospital I could find on the island of Honolulu but was unable to locate him, so the fear and sorrow continued.

I made arrangements to visit friends in California to get away, with one small shred of hope he might contact me and join me there.

Although I know I will survive if he no longer wants me in his life, I still have fear. I fear the reaction I had Wednesday. We have a second vacation scheduled in 2 weeks. I fear how I will deal with that emptiness, should things with him again fall through and I have to face that time alone. I don't know if I can take another disappointment and humiliation. I fear what I may feel prompted to do, to react, to feel compelled to do.

Part of each of these relationships turned into an obsession, not in the sense that I became insane or destructive, only self-destructive. For some reason, when I love someone, they become my world, so when the relationship falls apart, so do I, for I am nothing. I have never been more than nothing, nor do I anticipate ever being more than nothing. For this reason, I don't think I can ever allow myself to love again, can never trust any man to get that close. It is the only way to protect myself. Otherwise, I am afraid I will someday seek to destroy my own life.

I Honestly Don't Know

How does one survive the loss of their entire future?
We invest so much when we trust.
We give up a bit of ourselves.
We share our dreams, our hopes,
We plan a future around the life of anticipated love and
The building a new space in which each person has a greater self-worth.
And in a heartbeat it is gone.

Hopefully, our extended family unit is intact…our jobs are still in place,
Yet we seem to have nothing
Only pain
Where all the joy had been.

Heartache…pain…humiliation…loss.
How do I face those who had seen the shine in my face?
How do I face each new day knowing you won't be here?
It feels like the pain is too great
And will never end,
And how do I reconcile the feeling
That I am worthless?

I honestly don't know

Defining Love

How is it that people can profess love then walk away?
Love isn't a pencil that one can pick up and put down.

Love is like a brand.
It becomes a part of who we are.
It changes us and how we identify ourselves.
How we perceive ourselves through the joy it creates
and how others see us as we become more than we were.

By accepting the sweetness that another offers,
We are no longer the same person.
We grow, mature, season—
And as this process shapes us we become more unique
More kind, giving, loving.

The one defining characteristic I see of love
Is that it makes us someone who,
Because of the gifts we have given and received,
Does not want to go backwards…
Does not want to return to who and what we were before love arrived.

Shadows

I sit in silence...
I am crying...
I am alone...
Forty-five years ago, I lay in my bed in the dark
...in silence...crying...alone.
My father had just left the family and taken my sister with him.
My sister who he loved more than "the rest" of us.
My sister who I shared a room with.
I was left to return to my bed
...in the dark
...in silence
...crying
...alone
...unloved.
...unlovable
...nothing.

My life has gone full circle and I again sit in the same room
...alone.
No one knows I am here
No one cares

The silence cuts through my heart.
The tears burn my eyes.
The silence reinforces the fact that
no man on the face of the earth finds any value in me
I am alone.
I am nothing.

I desperately long to have another in my life to validate my existence

…someone who can see nothing

…someone who wants to fill my life with their presence

…someone who will light the dark corners of my mind, take my hand and guide me

out of my shadows

The Wish

I once knew passion.
It was warm and sweet
Because it was shared with one whom I loved.

Due to absence....or neglect
The passion,
like a sourdough starter without its regular infusion of nutrients
and attention,
Went flat.

Though the elements were still there…
Still one in mind
The effervescence was allowed to all but die
And the flame of love that once inspired went to coals…still
living but not alive.

Another came offering his touch—
The softness of his lips against my skin
The coals once again roared into a fire that threatened to consume.

How is it that the human body is so fickle
Accepting of comfort from any direction?
Unwilling or unable to reject passion that is offered
In the wake of loss…loneliness…pain?

Or is it the body's way of protecting our minds from drowning in
memory
Giving us one shred of hope to desperately cling to
That life will not always be thus.

It is not the loss of passion that is grieved for
It is the loss of love, companionship, friendship
For these are the things that are meant to last through time.

Passion comes and goes
But if all two have is passion then they have nothing
For passion cannot bind beyond itself.

Though my mind accepts offers of thoughts of shared passions
And the body may forget what was once accepted in love,
My soul will always carry an imprint of one who once touched my
mind AND my heart

The wish…I had been able to touch his.

Christmas

Oh what a child feels on Christmas morning.
Stockings filled with treats.
Always surprised.
A new day filled with hope…anticipation…
To see if we receive what we "always wanted."

I recall one Christmas having not written to Santa, or changing my mind last minute. I knelt by the side of my bed in prayer asking for a Little Red Spinning Wheel. No one had ever heard me indicate any desire for this toy, and since I hadn't communicated with Santa, I took it right to the top…to the Big Man.

Sunrise broke about the same time it always did. Why does Christmas morning seem longer than any other day of the year? We always had to wait until the parents were up to open our presents…but there were the stockings! And of course we had to inspect each and every present to find ours, evaluate by the sizes if there was anything worthwhile inside—or even better, what we truly wanted.

There was one box that might be…that could possibly be…the right size, but I had to be patient…

I am sure my brother, sisters and I enjoyed traditional fare…oranges, apples, nuts, chocolates…likely being well fed by the time mom and dad arrived at the bottom of the stairs.

We were unleashed! Without a hesitation or doubt, I went for the biggest box. Could it be the Little Red Spinning Wheel? IT WAS!!!!

At that moment, I knew…beyond the shadow of a doubt…that Santa Clause existed. He had to! That spinning wheel is still at my mom's house and brings back memories each time I see it.

The child learns…

it is okay to allow yourself to want good things.
hope is vital to a healthy life.
faith is a positive influence.
gratitude for good things.

The adult has learned…

There was someone who wanted me to have the best gift they could give…one they thought would make me happy. Someone wanted me to know that I was cared for, cherished, maybe even loved.

Measles

We see a small child with measles, for her own protection kept in a darkened room.
What they don't see is that this child...
  is alone...
  feels alone...unwanted.

Then, a sweet, sweet aunt returns from a shopping spree, comes to the child, places a robe around her back and sunglasses to protect her eyes, and takes her out of the darkness into the light. The aunt takes her into her room, and she models her new treasures, but the child knows she was given the greatest treasure of all...
  someone saw her in her loneliness...
  someone brought her into the light with their love.

The child learns...
  what it feels like to be totally alone...lost...nothing...
  what it feels like to be found...
  what it feels like to be loved...

The adult knows...
  feeling alone, lonely, lost is not something unnatural to a child who does not
  understand what is going on.

Given free reign, these things can consume our conscious mind, whether or not they are based in reality, fear, or false perceptions.

One has to accept that...
　　being lonely does not mean we will always be alone,
　　feeling lost does not mean we cannot or will not be found.

I Wish

I know how I felt about you when I let you go.
It's not that I didn't care for you
but I needed to know I was more to you
than just a convenience.

I wish you knew how often I think of you…
Your touch…the sound of your voice.
How often you are with me again
in the space of just one thought.

I hoped your skin, like mine, had a memory all its own,
The sensation of a gentle touch
yet passion beyond measure.
A kiss that in one instant
contained both restraint and freedom,
The strength and firmness of being kissed hard and long,
The sweetness and gentleness
that made us want to never stop.

My skin, too, longs for your touch…
to be held, for a moment, an hour, a day.
To feel your lips against my neck
while you nuzzle my earlobe.

I would wish you to remember me…
your lips remember the taste of my mouth…my skin,
your nose to remember the smell of my hair,
your mind repeatedly envisioning the time we spent,
the words spoken, the lives that touched.

My wish would be that you would find something simple and good, intelligent and strong, any part of our interaction that draws me back into your mind and creates a desire within you to have me a part of your life.

That would be my wish.

Communication

Silence…
Beating in my ears
Like a deafening, ever-accelerating drum

Silence…
Slicing open my mind,
Letting fear escape

Silence…
Cutting like a bullet
Through my heart

Silence…
Separating all things,
Seclusion
Total isolation

Communication…
Healing

Communication…
Resolving paranoia

Communication…
Calming, soothing

Communication…
Resolution

Communication…
Understanding…

Communication…
Empathy

Communication…
Respect

Communication…
"Commune"-ication…"commune"-ity

Silence…being one…alone
Communication…being one…together

To Heal

How can it be that when I am alone on a sunny day, sitting by a stream with the sun beating down on my face, and I am at peace…with myself and with God, I don't mind being alive. Yet the same person can sit here still as alone on a dark evening, sitting by the computer, lamp lighting the shadows, still okay with myself and God, I think, and I feel like it does not matter whether I live or not.

This is not an active wish to die, simply an acknowledgement of my lack of wish to live.
I have family…and friends…work…activities, things to occupy my hands, my mind, my heart; yet, when I think about the future I cry.

I do not feel afraid of the future, not even of being alone. I am working on my house,
have repaired lost or weakened relationships with my children. I play with my grandson and watch him grow and hope to soon hold a new spirit, as well as to hold my girls in my arms whose lives have gone a different direction. I don't get to see any of my children enough or hold them enough, but that is something I would lose if I were not alive.

Yet there is something within me that cries.

I try to remember a place or a time in my life where I was made to feel like my life had no value—I cannot.

I feel as hollow as the darkness seems.
I cannot see the light...
I cannot see a future.

I live my life in the present ever working toward the future...the condition of my home...the quality of my relationships...even attempting to tie my family past and present, living and dead. Yet, I must too look backward to see the foundation the present is built upon.

Sometimes, there are events, infinitessimal, that should hold no import, have no bearing on the present, yet those events sometimes leave deep impressions...yet not unalterable.
To heal the present, we have to heal the past. So I cast my eyes and my mind to a place...into the shadows to seek out that place within where the flame of hope went out,
by itself or with the efforts of another.

I want that light to burn, to draw out of the darkness the hope I once had so that I may see the way ahead and seek it with my whole being, leaving the darkness of my mind, for eternity only a shadow in the past, no longer a part of my present or a restraint from a future filled with all the love a heart can give.

Only in My Mind

We sit talking over dinner
I love learning about your life
the joys you have known
the tragedies you have seen.

While your face stays intense
absorbed in thought and word
My eyes become large with horror
then soften with the upturn of my lips
into a smile.

You intrigue me
You entrance me

We have talked many times on the phone,
but face to face
I see your strength and your courage,
I feel your compassion,
your love for your children, for history,
for life—
your passions.

You watch from the drive
as I stand under a tree gazing at the rain.
We share a ride, a scenic view,
a kiss.

After a firm back massage
(and you thought I would cause harm),

I gaze at your peacefully dozing face
as I gently, joyfully caress your feet.

We share an embrace,
undeniable passion,
and I go softly into the night
likely never to see you again.

Not fantasy by far,
neither something one can touch,
a part of me eternally,
for you are just a memory
I hold close and dear
yet, you are only in my mind.

Message to My Love…

I love your ability to sense when I need you.
You always know and you always come.
Your strong arms encompass me.
Your gentle breath soothes my spirit.

Have I ever told you how wonderful your laugh is?
Or how the small turn-up at the right corner of your mouth
gives away the secret mischief brewing beneath?

The touch of your hand is enough to wipe everything from my
mind…
except you.
In your embrace, I am aflame.

You are a gift.
One who is truly a blessing to my life,
and I cannot imagine one day without you.
With you, I look forward to each new sunrise
and to the end of each day for I know
you will be at my side in the day,
working together, building our life,
and at night we will lie in each other's arms,
sharing every part of ourselves until we at last
close our eyes in anticipation
of all our days yet to come.

I can think of no greater joy than spending my life with you,
unless it would be to be for us to be one for eternity.
You have so fully become a part of me, a part of my life,

opening your heart to me, trusting me
with your most intimate thoughts, fears, hopes, tears.

I know you are here…somewhere.
Heavenly Father has told me so.
Life has to this point kept us apart…strangers.
I long for the day when we will discover in ourselves
that part of us He made for each other.

I know…someday…I will hold you in my arms
as I hold you now with every hope in my heart.

A Perfect Me

Being perfect isn't a matter of not making mistakes and not having flaws.
It is more an acknowledgement of self, of who we are,
Who we want to be and how to attain it.

If I were perfect…

I would wake at sunrise and get out of bed, ready to grab the bull by the horns (if absolutely unavoidable) and proceed.

I would eat a healthy breakfast and use that time to write down my plans for the day, including some "me" time.

I would give thanks to Heavenly Father for another safe sojourn through the dark hours and for each blessing that I have (even those that feel more like curses).

I would join the rest of the human race in pursuing whatever livelihood I had with integrity, honesty and pride.

I would have the ability, skill, talent, what have you, to treat myself with at least as much respect as I would give another.

I would be able, in the midst of all my infirmities and challenges, to withstand the inherent weakness that threatens to degrade, debase, or destroy myself or others.

I would stand fast in my values, regardless of my fears. I would/ could not be swayed by the deprivations offered in the guise of false friendship or love.

I would not lay down my head to sleep until I had spoken with each of my children, so they know they are cherished.

I would reassess at the end of the day and look at whether I made the best use of my gifts on behalf of His other children.

As I knelt to give Him thanks for the day, I would ask for opportunities to serve, knowledge of how to better use my time and talents, courage to strengthen me in times of weakness, and wisdom to guide my every thought and action.

The Question

What I am to do with you?
You came into my life at a time
I was seeking connections, friendship.
You were willing to accept
The little I could offer of creature comfort.

Over time, though we have not touched since then,
Your needs have continued to grow
Until they encompass the whole
Of our communication.

You need so much more
Than I am comfortable giving of myself.
Yet I know there will never be
More between us than this,
A relationship only in the physical realm.
That is where our needs and wants part.

I have tried every so many times
To leave things in silence between us,
But even unspoken, the feelings exist.

My attraction to you is
No more emotional than yours to me.
We share a codependence,
Me feeding your need for someone
To communicate with sensually
To satisfy your need,
While feeding my inability to turn away

Your attentions solely because
You are attracted to me,
Want to be with me,
Possibly even need me,
Though I know my function is no more
Than any other woman on the planet.

I fear should the day come we do meet again,
That what little I am will be totally consumed
By your need, once again
Giving up any shred of dignity,
Self-respect, or hope for a different life.

I guess a better question is
What am I to do with myself?

Who Am I?

Who am I?
Am I simply what I think I am at this moment?
If so, I am nothing.
Not that I do not have value…
I have.
Not that I am without talent or gifts…
I am not.
Not that I am alone,
Without others in my life who care about me and I care about…
There are many.
I am nothing in the sense that
I am incapable of shaping or resisting
My future as far as relationships go.
I have the capacity to see
And the understanding to know when someone in my life
Is incapable of offering those things that I want and need…
Respect…compassion…emotional support.
I see and hear that their desires are not in line with my own life,
My choices, morality, comfort level,
Yet I am able to give little to no resistance
To the advances of their will, their wants, their needs,
To the subjection and even abandonment of my own.
I am not aware of a fear of being alone.
I do acknowledge though
That the men who have been in my life of late
Have wanted less and more of me.
Less of who I am, what I am, the life I lead,
More in the meeting of their own physical needs
Irrelevant of my own emotional and moral ones.

I have no hope of having a place
By anyone's side in the daylight
And fear I will lose myself altogether
If any of these long-distance fantasies
Are brought into my physical presence.
I have long prayed that there could be one in my life to
stem the tide,
To protect me from myself,
But alas there is no one.
So who or what am I?
I am alone, yet more afraid of who or what
I will become.

I Saw the Face of a Man

I saw the face of a man today.
He wasn't strikingly handsome by the world's standards
but there was definitely something about his face that gave me pause.

He was looking beyond me, though at that moment I could not
tell at what.
There was a twinkle to his eyes,
just the hint of a smile.
It gave me pleasure just to see.

As I gazed around the room beyond,
I noticed a party with many beautiful people.
Was his look one of a lover whose eyes locked with those of the
object of his affection?
I don't think so.

There was definitely a look of pleasure
and he gave the impression of being content to stand where he was,
to be an observer of the scene,
not needing to be an active participant.

As I took one last look before moving on,
I spied a wedding dress.
A young woman stood nearby, her face all aglow,
speaking enthusiastically with her guests.
She glanced around until her eyes settled on the groom on the far
side of the room.
A look of pure joy, peace, contentment decorated her delicate features.
She was truly a beautiful bride.

As I turned to continue my journey, I saw him again.
He was looking at a child, his child.
She had grown into a beautiful woman and was beginning her life
today.

I saw him smile as he caught her eye,
her smile once more just for him,
for the man who protected and nurtured her,
who loved her more than any man alive,
then she turned to take her husband's arm.

I saw the face of a man today.

No…

I saw the face of love today.

The Journey

As I travel down the path of my life, I see my destination in front
of me.
It gives me direction, keeps me focused.
It helps me to set priorities and make choices.
The desires of my heart also lead there,
Yet it feels like there ought to be more…
Someone to share the journey, to walk by my side, to contribute
to my life.

Too many times I have met people along the path
Who seem to be longing for the same destination as I.
I slow my path,
Sometimes coming to a full stop to invite them to join me.
We talk for a while, sometimes laugh, maybe cry together.
I continue on the journey
Only to eventually realize where there had been another,
There is now silence and I am once again alone.

Today, I have been blessed
With a new perspective, a new vision.

I can now see
That although their eyes may be fixed on the same destination
They are not always travelling at the same speed.
Sometimes not moving forward at all or choosing to take another
path.
Sometimes their paths are parallel,
Still with the same goal but having moved a ways off.

I can still see them, still desire to be with them,
But they cannot see me or have chosen
Not to share the path with me to reach the destination together.

So I continue on my journey,
Sometimes alone,
Yet still grateful to those who have given even one moment of
their time
To make my path a little brighter.

Will I be blessed to find someday one who chooses to share my
journey,
To work side by side, travel along the same path,
To attain the destination at the same time?
I hope so.
For I believe that this journey is not meant to be travelled alone,
And it is my hope that there is one who needs my companionship
As much as I need their's.